50 Homemade Milkshake Recipes for Home

By: Kelly Johnson

Table of Contents

- Classic Vanilla Milkshake
- Chocolate Lover's Milkshake
- Strawberry Dream Milkshake
- Peanut Butter Cup Milkshake
- Banana Cream Milkshake
- Oreo Cookie Milkshake
- Mint Chocolate Chip Milkshake
- Salted Caramel Milkshake
- Raspberry Swirl Milkshake
- Mocha Madness Milkshake
- Blueberry Blast Milkshake
- Cookies and Cream Milkshake
- Nutella Hazelnut Milkshake
- Cherry Cheesecake Milkshake
- Almond Joy Milkshake
- Pineapple Paradise Milkshake
- Coffee Toffee Milkshake
- Key Lime Pie Milkshake
- Rocky Road Milkshake
- Red Velvet Milkshake
- S'mores Milkshake
- Lemon Meringue Milkshake
- Cinnamon Roll Milkshake
- Mango Tango Milkshake
- Pistachio Delight Milkshake
- Brownie Batter Milkshake
- Peaches and Cream Milkshake
- Coconut Cream Pie Milkshake
- Maple Bacon Milkshake
- Black Forest Milkshake
- Pumpkin Spice Milkshake
- Caramel Apple Milkshake
- Birthday Cake Milkshake
- Snickerdoodle Milkshake
- Matcha Green Tea Milkshake

- Pina Colada Milkshake
- Raspberry Lemonade Milkshake
- Tiramisu Milkshake
- White Chocolate Raspberry Milkshake
- Orange Creamsicle Milkshake
- Eggnog Milkshake
- Honey Lavender Milkshake
- Caramel Macchiato Milkshake
- Chocolate Covered Strawberry Milkshake
- Maple Pecan Milkshake
- Peppermint Patty Milkshake
- Banana Split Milkshake
- Blue Moon Milkshake
- Lavender Honey Milkshake
- Irish Coffee Milkshake

Classic Vanilla Milkshake

Ingredients:

- 2 cups vanilla ice cream
- 1 cup whole milk
- 1 teaspoon vanilla extract
- Whipped cream (optional)
- Maraschino cherry for garnish (optional)

Instructions:

1. In a blender, combine the vanilla ice cream, whole milk, and vanilla extract.
2. Blend on high speed until smooth and creamy, about 30-60 seconds, depending on the blender.
3. If the milkshake is too thick, you can add a little more milk, a tablespoon at a time, until you reach your desired consistency.
4. Once blended, pour the milkshake into a chilled glass.
5. If desired, top with whipped cream and garnish with a maraschino cherry.
6. Serve immediately with a straw and enjoy your classic vanilla milkshake!

Chocolate Lover's Milkshake

Ingredients:

- 2 cups chocolate ice cream
- 1 cup whole milk
- 2 tablespoons chocolate syrup
- 2 tablespoons chocolate chips or chunks
- Whipped cream (optional)
- Chocolate shavings or sprinkles for garnish (optional)

Instructions:

1. In a blender, combine the chocolate ice cream, whole milk, chocolate syrup, and chocolate chips or chunks.
2. Blend on high speed until smooth and creamy, about 30-60 seconds.
3. If the milkshake is too thick, you can add a little more milk, a tablespoon at a time, until you reach your desired consistency.
4. Once blended, pour the chocolate milkshake into a chilled glass.
5. If desired, top with whipped cream and garnish with chocolate shavings or sprinkles.
6. Serve immediately with a straw and indulge in this decadent Chocolate Lover's Milkshake!

Strawberry Dream Milkshake

Ingredients:

- 2 cups strawberry ice cream
- 1 cup fresh or frozen strawberries, hulled
- 1 cup whole milk
- 2 tablespoons strawberry syrup (optional, for extra flavor)
- Whipped cream (optional)
- Fresh strawberries for garnish (optional)

Instructions:

1. In a blender, combine the strawberry ice cream, fresh or frozen strawberries, whole milk, and strawberry syrup (if using).
2. Blend on high speed until smooth and creamy, about 30-60 seconds.
3. If the milkshake is too thick, you can add a little more milk, a tablespoon at a time, until you reach your desired consistency.
4. Once blended, pour the strawberry milkshake into a chilled glass.
5. If desired, top with whipped cream and garnish with fresh strawberries.
6. Serve immediately with a straw and savor the delightful flavors of this Strawberry Dream Milkshake!

Peanut Butter Cup Milkshake

Ingredients:

- 2 cups chocolate ice cream
- 1 cup whole milk
- 2 tablespoons creamy peanut butter
- 2 tablespoons chocolate syrup
- 2-3 peanut butter cups, chopped (plus extra for garnish, optional)
- Whipped cream (optional)
- Chocolate shavings or sprinkles for garnish (optional)

Instructions:

1. In a blender, combine the chocolate ice cream, whole milk, creamy peanut butter, chocolate syrup, and chopped peanut butter cups.
2. Blend on high speed until smooth and creamy, about 30-60 seconds.
3. If the milkshake is too thick, you can add a little more milk, a tablespoon at a time, until you reach your desired consistency.
4. Once blended, pour the peanut butter cup milkshake into a chilled glass.
5. If desired, top with whipped cream and garnish with additional chopped peanut butter cups, chocolate shavings, or sprinkles.
6. Serve immediately with a straw and enjoy the irresistible flavor combination of chocolate and peanut butter in this Peanut Butter Cup Milkshake!

Banana Cream Milkshake

Ingredients:

- 2 ripe bananas, sliced and frozen
- 2 cups vanilla ice cream
- 1 cup whole milk
- 1 teaspoon vanilla extract
- Whipped cream (optional)
- Sliced bananas for garnish (optional)
- Crushed vanilla wafer cookies for garnish (optional)

Instructions:

1. In a blender, add the frozen banana slices, vanilla ice cream, whole milk, and vanilla extract.
2. Blend on high speed until smooth and creamy, about 30-60 seconds.
3. If the milkshake is too thick, you can add a little more milk, a tablespoon at a time, until you reach your desired consistency.
4. Once blended, pour the banana cream milkshake into chilled glasses.
5. If desired, top each milkshake with a dollop of whipped cream.
6. Garnish with sliced bananas and crushed vanilla wafer cookies for an extra touch of flavor and texture.
7. Serve immediately with a straw and enjoy the creamy, banana goodness of this Banana Cream Milkshake!

Oreo Cookie Milkshake

Ingredients:

- 2 cups vanilla ice cream
- 1 cup whole milk
- 4-6 Oreo cookies, plus extra for garnish (optional)
- 2 tablespoons chocolate syrup
- Whipped cream (optional)

Instructions:

1. In a blender, combine the vanilla ice cream, whole milk, Oreo cookies, and chocolate syrup.
2. Blend on high speed until the cookies are fully crushed and the mixture is smooth and creamy, about 30-60 seconds.
3. If the milkshake is too thick, you can add a little more milk, a tablespoon at a time, until you reach your desired consistency.
4. Once blended, pour the Oreo cookie milkshake into chilled glasses.
5. If desired, top each milkshake with a dollop of whipped cream and garnish with additional Oreo cookie crumbles.
6. Serve immediately with a straw and enjoy the classic cookies and cream flavor of this Oreo Cookie Milkshake!

Mint Chocolate Chip Milkshake

Ingredients:

- 2 cups mint chocolate chip ice cream
- 1 cup whole milk
- 1/4 teaspoon peppermint extract (optional, for extra minty flavor)
- 1/4 cup chocolate chips or chunks
- Green food coloring (optional, for a more vibrant green color)
- Whipped cream (optional)
- Chocolate shavings or mint leaves for garnish (optional)

Instructions:

1. In a blender, combine the mint chocolate chip ice cream, whole milk, peppermint extract (if using), and chocolate chips or chunks.
2. Optional: Add a few drops of green food coloring for a more vibrant green color.
3. Blend on high speed until smooth and creamy, about 30-60 seconds.
4. If the milkshake is too thick, you can add a little more milk, a tablespoon at a time, until you reach your desired consistency.
5. Once blended, pour the mint chocolate chip milkshake into chilled glasses.
6. If desired, top each milkshake with whipped cream and garnish with chocolate shavings or mint leaves.
7. Serve immediately with a straw and enjoy the refreshing and indulgent flavor of this Mint Chocolate Chip Milkshake!

Salted Caramel Milkshake

Ingredients:

- 2 cups vanilla ice cream
- 1 cup whole milk
- 1/4 cup caramel sauce, plus extra for drizzling
- 1/2 teaspoon sea salt
- Whipped cream (optional)
- Caramel candies or caramel popcorn for garnish (optional)

Instructions:

1. In a blender, combine the vanilla ice cream, whole milk, caramel sauce, and sea salt.
2. Blend on high speed until smooth and creamy, about 30-60 seconds.
3. If the milkshake is too thick, you can add a little more milk, a tablespoon at a time, until you reach your desired consistency.
4. Once blended, drizzle some caramel sauce inside the glasses before pouring in the milkshake mixture.
5. Pour the salted caramel milkshake into chilled glasses.
6. If desired, top each milkshake with whipped cream and garnish with additional drizzles of caramel sauce and caramel candies or caramel popcorn.
7. Serve immediately with a straw and savor the rich, sweet, and slightly salty flavor of this Salted Caramel Milkshake!

Raspberry Swirl Milkshake

Ingredients:

- 2 cups vanilla ice cream
- 1 cup whole milk
- 1 cup fresh or frozen raspberries
- 2 tablespoons raspberry syrup or raspberry preserves
- Whipped cream (optional)
- Fresh raspberries for garnish (optional)

Instructions:

1. In a blender, combine the vanilla ice cream, whole milk, fresh or frozen raspberries, and raspberry syrup or preserves.
2. Blend on high speed until smooth and creamy, about 30-60 seconds.
3. If the milkshake is too thick, you can add a little more milk, a tablespoon at a time, until you reach your desired consistency.
4. Once blended, pour the raspberry swirl milkshake into chilled glasses.
5. If desired, top each milkshake with whipped cream and garnish with fresh raspberries.
6. Serve immediately with a straw and enjoy the refreshing and fruity flavor of this Raspberry Swirl Milkshake!

Mocha Madness Milkshake

Ingredients:

- 2 cups coffee ice cream
- 1 cup whole milk
- 2 tablespoons chocolate syrup
- 1 tablespoon instant espresso powder or coffee granules
- Whipped cream (optional)
- Chocolate shavings or cocoa powder for garnish (optional)

Instructions:

1. In a blender, combine the coffee ice cream, whole milk, chocolate syrup, and instant espresso powder or coffee granules.
2. Blend on high speed until smooth and creamy, about 30-60 seconds.
3. If the milkshake is too thick, you can add a little more milk, a tablespoon at a time, until you reach your desired consistency.
4. Once blended, pour the mocha madness milkshake into chilled glasses.
5. If desired, top each milkshake with whipped cream and garnish with chocolate shavings or cocoa powder.
6. Serve immediately with a straw and enjoy the rich and indulgent flavor of this Mocha Madness Milkshake!

Blueberry Blast Milkshake

Ingredients:

- 2 cups vanilla ice cream
- 1 cup whole milk
- 1 cup fresh or frozen blueberries
- 2 tablespoons honey or maple syrup
- 1 teaspoon vanilla extract
- Whipped cream (optional)
- Fresh blueberries for garnish (optional)

Instructions:

1. In a blender, combine the vanilla ice cream, whole milk, fresh or frozen blueberries, honey or maple syrup, and vanilla extract.
2. Blend on high speed until smooth and creamy, about 30-60 seconds.
3. If the milkshake is too thick, you can add a little more milk, a tablespoon at a time, until you reach your desired consistency.
4. Once blended, pour the blueberry blast milkshake into chilled glasses.
5. If desired, top each milkshake with whipped cream and garnish with fresh blueberries.
6. Serve immediately with a straw and enjoy the refreshing and fruity flavor of this Blueberry Blast Milkshake!

Cookies and Cream Milkshake

Ingredients:

- 2 cups vanilla ice cream
- 1 cup whole milk
- 6-8 chocolate sandwich cookies (such as Oreos), plus extra for garnish (optional)
- 2 tablespoons chocolate syrup
- Whipped cream (optional)

Instructions:

1. In a blender, combine the vanilla ice cream, whole milk, and chocolate sandwich cookies.
2. Add the chocolate syrup.
3. Blend on high speed until smooth and creamy, about 30-60 seconds.
4. If the milkshake is too thick, you can add a little more milk, a tablespoon at a time, until you reach your desired consistency.
5. Once blended, pour the cookies and cream milkshake into chilled glasses.
6. If desired, top each milkshake with whipped cream and garnish with additional crushed chocolate sandwich cookies.
7. Serve immediately with a straw and enjoy the classic flavor of this Cookies and Cream Milkshake!

Nutella Hazelnut Milkshake

Ingredients:

- 2 cups vanilla ice cream
- 1 cup whole milk
- 1/4 cup Nutella (or more to taste)
- 1/4 cup chopped hazelnuts, toasted (optional, for garnish)
- Whipped cream (optional)
- Chocolate shavings or cocoa powder for garnish (optional)

Instructions:

1. In a blender, combine the vanilla ice cream, whole milk, and Nutella.
2. Blend on high speed until smooth and creamy, about 30-60 seconds.
3. If the milkshake is too thick, you can add a little more milk, a tablespoon at a time, until you reach your desired consistency.
4. Once blended, pour the Nutella hazelnut milkshake into chilled glasses.
5. If desired, top each milkshake with whipped cream and garnish with chopped toasted hazelnuts, chocolate shavings, or cocoa powder.
6. Serve immediately with a straw and enjoy the delicious combination of Nutella and hazelnuts in this Nutella Hazelnut Milkshake!

Cherry Cheesecake Milkshake

Ingredients:

- 2 cups vanilla ice cream
- 1 cup whole milk
- 1/2 cup cherry pie filling
- 2 ounces cream cheese, softened
- 1 teaspoon vanilla extract
- Graham cracker crumbs for garnish
- Whipped cream (optional)
- Maraschino cherries for garnish (optional)

Instructions:

1. In a blender, combine the vanilla ice cream, whole milk, cherry pie filling, softened cream cheese, and vanilla extract.
2. Blend on high speed until smooth and creamy, about 30-60 seconds.
3. If the milkshake is too thick, you can add a little more milk, a tablespoon at a time, until you reach your desired consistency.
4. Once blended, pour the cherry cheesecake milkshake into chilled glasses.
5. If desired, top each milkshake with whipped cream and garnish with graham cracker crumbs and a maraschino cherry.
6. Serve immediately with a straw and enjoy the delightful flavors of this Cherry Cheesecake Milkshake!

Almond Joy Milkshake

Ingredients:

- 2 cups chocolate ice cream
- 1 cup whole milk
- 1/4 cup shredded coconut
- 2 tablespoons chocolate syrup
- 2 tablespoons almond butter
- 1/4 cup chopped almonds
- Whipped cream (optional)
- Shredded coconut and chopped almonds for garnish (optional)

Instructions:

1. In a blender, combine the chocolate ice cream, whole milk, shredded coconut, chocolate syrup, almond butter, and chopped almonds.
2. Blend on high speed until smooth and creamy, about 30-60 seconds.
3. If the milkshake is too thick, you can add a little more milk, a tablespoon at a time, until you reach your desired consistency.
4. Once blended, pour the Almond Joy milkshake into chilled glasses.
5. If desired, top each milkshake with whipped cream and garnish with shredded coconut and chopped almonds.
6. Serve immediately with a straw and enjoy the indulgent flavors of this Almond Joy Milkshake!

Pineapple Paradise Milkshake

Ingredients:

- 2 cups vanilla ice cream
- 1 cup pineapple chunks, fresh or canned (drained)
- 1/2 cup pineapple juice
- 1/4 cup coconut milk
- 2 tablespoons honey or sugar (adjust to taste)
- Optional: 1 tablespoon shredded coconut for garnish
- Optional: Pineapple slices for garnish

Instructions:

1. In a blender, combine the vanilla ice cream, pineapple chunks, pineapple juice, coconut milk, and honey or sugar.
2. Blend on high speed until smooth and creamy, about 30-60 seconds.
3. Taste and adjust sweetness if needed by adding more honey or sugar.
4. If the milkshake is too thick, you can add a little more pineapple juice or coconut milk, a tablespoon at a time, until you reach your desired consistency.
5. Once blended, pour the Pineapple Paradise milkshake into chilled glasses.
6. If desired, garnish with shredded coconut and a pineapple slice on the rim of the glass.
7. Serve immediately with a straw and enjoy the tropical bliss of this Pineapple Paradise Milkshake!

Coffee Toffee Milkshake

Ingredients:

- 2 cups coffee ice cream
- 1 cup whole milk
- 2 tablespoons toffee syrup or sauce
- 1 tablespoon instant coffee powder (adjust to taste)
- 2 tablespoons crushed toffee candy or Heath bar
- Whipped cream (optional)
- Crushed toffee candy for garnish (optional)

Instructions:

1. In a blender, combine the coffee ice cream, whole milk, toffee syrup or sauce, and instant coffee powder.
2. Blend on high speed until smooth and creamy, about 30-60 seconds.
3. Taste and adjust the intensity of coffee flavor by adding more instant coffee powder if desired.
4. Once blended, add the crushed toffee candy or Heath bar and pulse a few times to incorporate it into the milkshake while still leaving some small chunks for texture.
5. Pour the Coffee Toffee milkshake into chilled glasses.
6. If desired, top each milkshake with whipped cream and garnish with crushed toffee candy.
7. Serve immediately with a straw and enjoy the rich coffee and toffee flavors of this indulgent Coffee Toffee Milkshake!

Key Lime Pie Milkshake

Ingredients:

- 2 cups vanilla ice cream
- 1 cup whole milk
- 1/4 cup key lime juice
- 1 tablespoon lime zest
- 2 tablespoons sweetened condensed milk
- 2 graham crackers, crushed
- Whipped cream (optional)
- Lime slices for garnish (optional)

Instructions:

1. In a blender, combine the vanilla ice cream, whole milk, key lime juice, lime zest, and sweetened condensed milk.
2. Blend on high speed until smooth and creamy, about 30-60 seconds.
3. Taste and adjust the sweetness or tanginess by adding more sweetened condensed milk or lime juice, if desired.
4. Once blended, add the crushed graham crackers and pulse a few times to incorporate them into the milkshake while still leaving some texture.
5. Pour the Key Lime Pie milkshake into chilled glasses.
6. If desired, top each milkshake with whipped cream and garnish with a lime slice.
7. Serve immediately with a straw and enjoy the refreshing and tangy flavors of this Key Lime Pie Milkshake!

Rocky Road Milkshake

Ingredients:

- 2 cups chocolate ice cream
- 1 cup whole milk
- 1/4 cup chopped almonds
- 1/4 cup mini marshmallows
- 2 tablespoons chocolate syrup
- Whipped cream (optional)
- Chocolate shavings for garnish (optional)

Instructions:

1. In a blender, combine the chocolate ice cream, whole milk, chopped almonds, mini marshmallows, and chocolate syrup.
2. Blend on high speed until smooth and creamy, about 30-60 seconds.
3. If the milkshake is too thick, you can add a little more milk, a tablespoon at a time, until you reach your desired consistency.
4. Once blended, pour the Rocky Road milkshake into chilled glasses.
5. If desired, top each milkshake with whipped cream and garnish with chocolate shavings.
6. Serve immediately with a straw and enjoy the delightful combination of chocolate, almonds, and marshmallows in this Rocky Road Milkshake!

Red Velvet Milkshake

Ingredients:

- 2 cups red velvet cake ice cream
- 1 cup whole milk
- 1/2 cup cream cheese, softened
- 2 tablespoons cocoa powder
- 1/4 cup powdered sugar (adjust to taste)
- Red food coloring (optional, for a deeper red color)
- Whipped cream (optional)
- Red velvet cake crumbs for garnish (optional)

Instructions:

1. In a blender, combine the red velvet cake ice cream, whole milk, softened cream cheese, cocoa powder, and powdered sugar.
2. Add a few drops of red food coloring if you want a deeper red color.
3. Blend on high speed until smooth and creamy, about 30-60 seconds.
4. Taste and adjust sweetness by adding more powdered sugar if desired.
5. If the milkshake is too thick, you can add a little more milk, a tablespoon at a time, until you reach your desired consistency.
6. Once blended, pour the Red Velvet milkshake into chilled glasses.
7. If desired, top each milkshake with whipped cream and garnish with red velvet cake crumbs.
8. Serve immediately with a straw and enjoy the rich and indulgent flavor of this Red Velvet Milkshake!

S'mores Milkshake

Ingredients:

- 2 cups chocolate ice cream
- 1 cup whole milk
- 2 tablespoons chocolate syrup
- 2 tablespoons marshmallow fluff or marshmallow creme
- 2 graham crackers, crushed
- Whipped cream (optional)
- Mini marshmallows and chocolate shavings for garnish (optional)

Instructions:

1. In a blender, combine the chocolate ice cream, whole milk, chocolate syrup, and marshmallow fluff.
2. Blend on high speed until smooth and creamy, about 30-60 seconds.
3. If the milkshake is too thick, you can add a little more milk, a tablespoon at a time, until you reach your desired consistency.
4. Once blended, add half of the crushed graham crackers to the blender and pulse a few times to incorporate them into the milkshake while still leaving some texture.
5. Pour the S'mores milkshake into chilled glasses.
6. If desired, top each milkshake with whipped cream and garnish with mini marshmallows, chocolate shavings, and the remaining crushed graham crackers.
7. Serve immediately with a straw and enjoy the nostalgic flavors of this S'mores Milkshake!

Lemon Meringue Milkshake

Ingredients:

- 2 cups lemon sorbet or lemon ice cream
- 1 cup whole milk
- 1/4 cup lemon curd
- 1 teaspoon lemon zest
- 1 tablespoon powdered sugar (optional, adjust to taste)
- Whipped cream (optional)
- Toasted meringue or meringue cookies for garnish (optional)

Instructions:

1. In a blender, combine the lemon sorbet or lemon ice cream, whole milk, lemon curd, lemon zest, and powdered sugar (if using).
2. Blend on high speed until smooth and creamy, about 30-60 seconds.
3. Taste and adjust sweetness by adding more powdered sugar if desired.
4. If the milkshake is too thick, you can add a little more milk, a tablespoon at a time, until you reach your desired consistency.
5. Once blended, pour the Lemon Meringue milkshake into chilled glasses.
6. If desired, top each milkshake with whipped cream and garnish with toasted meringue or meringue cookies.
7. Serve immediately with a straw and enjoy the refreshing and tangy flavor of this Lemon Meringue Milkshake!

Cinnamon Roll Milkshake

Ingredients:

- 2 cups vanilla ice cream
- 1 cup whole milk
- 2 tablespoons cinnamon sugar
- 1/4 cup cream cheese, softened
- 1 teaspoon vanilla extract
- Whipped cream (optional)
- Cinnamon sugar for garnish (optional)
- Cinnamon sticks for garnish (optional)

Instructions:

1. In a blender, combine the vanilla ice cream, whole milk, cinnamon sugar, softened cream cheese, and vanilla extract.
2. Blend on high speed until smooth and creamy, about 30-60 seconds.
3. Taste and adjust sweetness or cinnamon flavor by adding more cinnamon sugar if desired.
4. If the milkshake is too thick, you can add a little more milk, a tablespoon at a time, until you reach your desired consistency.
5. Once blended, pour the Cinnamon Roll milkshake into chilled glasses.
6. If desired, top each milkshake with whipped cream and sprinkle with cinnamon sugar.
7. Garnish with cinnamon sticks for an extra touch.
8. Serve immediately with a straw and enjoy the comforting flavors of this Cinnamon Roll Milkshake!

Mango Tango Milkshake

Ingredients:

- 2 cups mango sorbet or frozen mango chunks
- 1 cup vanilla ice cream
- 1 cup whole milk
- 1 tablespoon honey or sugar (optional, adjust to taste)
- 1/2 teaspoon vanilla extract
- Optional: a squeeze of lime juice for extra tanginess
- Whipped cream (optional)
- Sliced mango or mint leaves for garnish (optional)

Instructions:

1. In a blender, combine the mango sorbet or frozen mango chunks, vanilla ice cream, whole milk, honey or sugar (if using), and vanilla extract.
2. Optional: Add a squeeze of lime juice for an extra tangy kick.
3. Blend on high speed until smooth and creamy, about 30-60 seconds.
4. Taste and adjust sweetness by adding more honey or sugar if desired.
5. If the milkshake is too thick, you can add a little more milk, a tablespoon at a time, until you reach your desired consistency.
6. Once blended, pour the Mango Tango milkshake into chilled glasses.
7. If desired, top each milkshake with whipped cream and garnish with sliced mango or mint leaves.
8. Serve immediately with a straw and enjoy the tropical flavors of this Mango Tango Milkshake!

Pistachio Delight Milkshake

Ingredients:

- 2 cups pistachio ice cream
- 1 cup whole milk
- 1/4 cup shelled pistachios, chopped
- 1 tablespoon honey or sugar (optional, adjust to taste)
- 1/4 teaspoon almond extract (optional, for extra flavor)
- Whipped cream (optional)
- Chopped pistachios for garnish (optional)

Instructions:

1. In a blender, combine the pistachio ice cream, whole milk, chopped pistachios, honey or sugar (if using), and almond extract (if using).
2. Blend on high speed until smooth and creamy, about 30-60 seconds.
3. Taste and adjust sweetness by adding more honey or sugar if desired.
4. If the milkshake is too thick, you can add a little more milk, a tablespoon at a time, until you reach your desired consistency.
5. Once blended, pour the Pistachio Delight milkshake into chilled glasses.
6. If desired, top each milkshake with whipped cream and garnish with chopped pistachios.
7. Serve immediately with a straw and enjoy the nutty and creamy flavors of this Pistachio Delight Milkshake!

Brownie Batter Milkshake

Ingredients:

- 2 cups chocolate ice cream
- 1 cup whole milk
- 1/4 cup brownie mix (dry mix, not prepared)
- 2 tablespoons chocolate syrup
- 1/4 cup mini chocolate chips
- Whipped cream (optional)
- Crushed brownie pieces for garnish (optional)

Instructions:

1. In a blender, combine the chocolate ice cream, whole milk, brownie mix, chocolate syrup, and mini chocolate chips.
2. Blend on high speed until smooth and creamy, about 30-60 seconds.
3. If the milkshake is too thick, you can add a little more milk, a tablespoon at a time, until you reach your desired consistency.
4. Once blended, pour the Brownie Batter milkshake into chilled glasses.
5. If desired, top each milkshake with whipped cream and garnish with crushed brownie pieces.
6. Serve immediately with a straw and enjoy the rich and indulgent flavors of this Brownie Batter Milkshake!

Peaches and Cream Milkshake

Ingredients:

- 2 cups vanilla ice cream
- 1 cup fresh or frozen peaches, sliced
- 1/2 cup whole milk
- 2 tablespoons honey or sugar (adjust to taste)
- 1/4 teaspoon vanilla extract
- Whipped cream (optional)
- Sliced peaches for garnish (optional)

Instructions:

1. In a blender, combine the vanilla ice cream, fresh or frozen peaches, whole milk, honey or sugar, and vanilla extract.
2. Blend on high speed until smooth and creamy, about 30-60 seconds.
3. Taste and adjust sweetness by adding more honey or sugar if desired.
4. If the milkshake is too thick, you can add a little more milk, a tablespoon at a time, until you reach your desired consistency.
5. Once blended, pour the Peaches and Cream milkshake into chilled glasses.
6. If desired, top each milkshake with whipped cream and garnish with sliced peaches.
7. Serve immediately with a straw and enjoy the refreshing and fruity flavors of this Peaches and Cream Milkshake!

Coconut Cream Pie Milkshake

Ingredients:

- 2 cups vanilla ice cream
- 1 cup coconut milk
- 1/4 cup sweetened shredded coconut
- 2 tablespoons coconut cream (optional, for extra coconut flavor)
- 2 tablespoons graham cracker crumbs
- 1 tablespoon powdered sugar (optional, adjust to taste)
- Whipped cream (optional)
- Toasted coconut flakes for garnish (optional)

Instructions:

1. In a blender, combine the vanilla ice cream, coconut milk, sweetened shredded coconut, coconut cream (if using), graham cracker crumbs, and powdered sugar (if using).
2. Blend on high speed until smooth and creamy, about 30-60 seconds.
3. Taste and adjust sweetness by adding more powdered sugar if desired.
4. If the milkshake is too thick, you can add a little more coconut milk, a tablespoon at a time, until you reach your desired consistency.
5. Once blended, pour the Coconut Cream Pie milkshake into chilled glasses.
6. If desired, top each milkshake with whipped cream and garnish with toasted coconut flakes.
7. Serve immediately with a straw and enjoy the tropical and creamy flavors of this Coconut Cream Pie Milkshake!

Maple Bacon Milkshake

Ingredients:

- 2 cups vanilla ice cream
- 1 cup whole milk
- 4 strips of bacon, cooked and crispy
- 2 tablespoons maple syrup
- 1/2 teaspoon vanilla extract
- Whipped cream (optional)
- Additional crispy bacon pieces for garnish (optional)

Instructions:

1. In a blender, combine the vanilla ice cream, whole milk, crispy bacon strips, maple syrup, and vanilla extract.
2. Blend on high speed until the bacon is finely chopped and the mixture is smooth and creamy, about 30-60 seconds.
3. Taste and adjust sweetness by adding more maple syrup if desired.
4. If the milkshake is too thick, you can add a little more milk, a tablespoon at a time, until you reach your desired consistency.
5. Once blended, pour the Maple Bacon milkshake into chilled glasses.
6. If desired, top each milkshake with whipped cream and garnish with additional crispy bacon pieces.
7. Serve immediately with a straw and enjoy the unique and delicious combination of sweet maple and savory bacon flavors in this Maple Bacon Milkshake!

Black Forest Milkshake

Ingredients:

- 2 cups chocolate ice cream
- 1 cup pitted cherries (fresh or frozen)
- 1 cup whole milk
- 2 tablespoons chocolate syrup
- 1 tablespoon cherry liqueur (optional)
- Whipped cream (optional)
- Chocolate shavings for garnish (optional)
- Maraschino cherries for garnish (optional)

Instructions:

1. In a blender, combine the chocolate ice cream, pitted cherries, whole milk, chocolate syrup, and cherry liqueur (if using).
2. Blend on high speed until smooth and creamy, about 30-60 seconds.
3. Taste and adjust sweetness or cherry flavor by adding more chocolate syrup or cherries if desired.
4. If the milkshake is too thick, you can add a little more milk, a tablespoon at a time, until you reach your desired consistency.
5. Once blended, pour the Black Forest milkshake into chilled glasses.
6. If desired, top each milkshake with whipped cream and garnish with chocolate shavings and a maraschino cherry.
7. Serve immediately with a straw and enjoy the rich and decadent flavors of this Black Forest Milkshake!

Pumpkin Spice Milkshake

Ingredients:

- 2 cups vanilla ice cream
- 1/2 cup pumpkin puree
- 1 cup whole milk
- 2 tablespoons maple syrup or honey
- 1 teaspoon pumpkin pie spice
- Whipped cream (optional)
- Ground cinnamon for garnish (optional)

Instructions:

1. In a blender, combine the vanilla ice cream, pumpkin puree, whole milk, maple syrup or honey, and pumpkin pie spice.
2. Blend on high speed until smooth and creamy, about 30-60 seconds.
3. Taste and adjust sweetness or spice level by adding more maple syrup or pumpkin pie spice if desired.
4. If the milkshake is too thick, you can add a little more milk, a tablespoon at a time, until you reach your desired consistency.
5. Once blended, pour the Pumpkin Spice milkshake into chilled glasses.
6. If desired, top each milkshake with whipped cream and garnish with a sprinkle of ground cinnamon.
7. Serve immediately with a straw and enjoy the cozy flavors of this Pumpkin Spice Milkshake!

Caramel Apple Milkshake

Ingredients:

- 2 cups vanilla ice cream
- 1 cup apple cider
- 1 apple, peeled, cored, and chopped
- 2 tablespoons caramel sauce, plus extra for drizzling
- 1/2 teaspoon ground cinnamon
- Whipped cream (optional)
- Cinnamon sticks for garnish (optional)

Instructions:

1. In a blender, combine the vanilla ice cream, apple cider, chopped apple, caramel sauce, and ground cinnamon.
2. Blend on high speed until smooth and creamy, about 30-60 seconds.
3. Taste and adjust sweetness or spice level by adding more caramel sauce or ground cinnamon if desired.
4. If the milkshake is too thick, you can add a little more apple cider, a tablespoon at a time, until you reach your desired consistency.
5. Once blended, drizzle caramel sauce inside the glasses before pouring in the milkshake mixture.
6. Pour the Caramel Apple milkshake into chilled glasses.
7. If desired, top each milkshake with whipped cream and garnish with a drizzle of caramel sauce and a cinnamon stick.
8. Serve immediately with a straw and enjoy the delightful flavors of this Caramel Apple Milkshake!

Birthday Cake Milkshake

Ingredients:

- 2 cups vanilla ice cream
- 1 cup whole milk
- 1/2 cup yellow cake mix (dry mix, not prepared)
- 2 tablespoons rainbow sprinkles
- 1 teaspoon vanilla extract
- Whipped cream (optional)
- Additional rainbow sprinkles for garnish (optional)

Instructions:

1. In a blender, combine the vanilla ice cream, whole milk, yellow cake mix, rainbow sprinkles, and vanilla extract.
2. Blend on high speed until smooth and creamy, about 30-60 seconds.
3. If the milkshake is too thick, you can add a little more milk, a tablespoon at a time, until you reach your desired consistency.
4. Once blended, pour the Birthday Cake milkshake into chilled glasses.
5. If desired, top each milkshake with whipped cream and garnish with additional rainbow sprinkles.
6. Serve immediately with a straw and enjoy the festive flavors of this Birthday Cake Milkshake!

Snickerdoodle Milkshake

Ingredients:

- 2 cups vanilla ice cream
- 1 cup whole milk
- 2 tablespoons snickerdoodle cookie butter or spread
- 1 tablespoon ground cinnamon
- 1 teaspoon vanilla extract
- Whipped cream (optional)
- Cinnamon sugar for garnish (optional)

Instructions:

1. In a blender, combine the vanilla ice cream, whole milk, snickerdoodle cookie butter or spread, ground cinnamon, and vanilla extract.
2. Blend on high speed until smooth and creamy, about 30-60 seconds.
3. Taste and adjust sweetness or cinnamon flavor by adding more snickerdoodle cookie butter or ground cinnamon if desired.
4. If the milkshake is too thick, you can add a little more milk, a tablespoon at a time, until you reach your desired consistency.
5. Once blended, pour the Snickerdoodle milkshake into chilled glasses.
6. If desired, top each milkshake with whipped cream and garnish with a sprinkle of cinnamon sugar.
7. Serve immediately with a straw and enjoy the delicious flavors of this Snickerdoodle Milkshake!

Matcha Green Tea Milkshake

Ingredients:

- 2 cups vanilla ice cream
- 1 cup whole milk
- 2 teaspoons matcha green tea powder
- 2 tablespoons honey or sugar (adjust to taste)
- 1/2 teaspoon vanilla extract
- Whipped cream (optional)
- Matcha powder for garnish (optional)

Instructions:

1. In a blender, combine the vanilla ice cream, whole milk, matcha green tea powder, honey or sugar, and vanilla extract.
2. Blend on high speed until the matcha powder is fully incorporated and the mixture is smooth and creamy, about 30-60 seconds.
3. Taste and adjust sweetness by adding more honey or sugar if desired.
4. If the milkshake is too thick, you can add a little more milk, a tablespoon at a time, until you reach your desired consistency.
5. Once blended, pour the Matcha Green Tea milkshake into chilled glasses.
6. If desired, top each milkshake with whipped cream and garnish with a sprinkle of matcha powder.
7. Serve immediately with a straw and enjoy the refreshing and vibrant flavors of this Matcha Green Tea Milkshake!

Pina Colada Milkshake

Ingredients:

- 2 cups vanilla ice cream
- 1 cup canned pineapple chunks, drained
- 1/2 cup coconut milk
- 1/4 cup pineapple juice
- 2 tablespoons coconut cream or cream of coconut
- 2 tablespoons white rum (optional)
- 1 tablespoon honey or sugar (optional, adjust to taste)
- Pineapple slices and maraschino cherries for garnish (optional)

Instructions:

1. In a blender, combine the vanilla ice cream, canned pineapple chunks, coconut milk, pineapple juice, coconut cream or cream of coconut, and white rum (if using).
2. Blend on high speed until smooth and creamy, about 30-60 seconds.
3. Taste and adjust sweetness by adding honey or sugar if desired.
4. If the milkshake is too thick, you can add a little more coconut milk or pineapple juice, a tablespoon at a time, until you reach your desired consistency.
5. Once blended, pour the Pina Colada milkshake into chilled glasses.
6. If desired, garnish each milkshake with a pineapple slice and a maraschino cherry.
7. Serve immediately with a straw and enjoy the tropical flavors of this Pina Colada Milkshake!

Raspberry Lemonade Milkshake

Ingredients:

- 2 cups vanilla ice cream
- 1 cup frozen raspberries
- 1/2 cup lemonade
- 1 tablespoon lemon zest
- 1-2 tablespoons honey or sugar (adjust to taste)
- Whipped cream (optional)
- Fresh raspberries for garnish (optional)
- Lemon slices for garnish (optional)

Instructions:

1. In a blender, combine the vanilla ice cream, frozen raspberries, lemonade, lemon zest, and honey or sugar.
2. Blend on high speed until smooth and creamy, about 30-60 seconds.
3. Taste and adjust sweetness by adding more honey or sugar if desired.
4. If the milkshake is too thick, you can add a little more lemonade, a tablespoon at a time, until you reach your desired consistency.
5. Once blended, pour the Raspberry Lemonade milkshake into chilled glasses.
6. If desired, top each milkshake with whipped cream and garnish with fresh raspberries and lemon slices.
7. Serve immediately with a straw and enjoy the refreshing and tangy flavors of this Raspberry Lemonade Milkshake!

Tiramisu Milkshake

Ingredients:

- 2 cups vanilla ice cream
- 1 cup brewed espresso or strong coffee, cooled
- 1/4 cup mascarpone cheese
- 2 tablespoons coffee liqueur (such as Kahlua)
- 1 tablespoon cocoa powder
- 1 tablespoon powdered sugar (adjust to taste)
- Ladyfingers, crushed (optional, for garnish)
- Whipped cream (optional)
- Cocoa powder or chocolate shavings for garnish (optional)

Instructions:

1. In a blender, combine the vanilla ice cream, brewed espresso or strong coffee, mascarpone cheese, coffee liqueur, cocoa powder, and powdered sugar.
2. Blend on high speed until smooth and creamy, about 30-60 seconds.
3. Taste and adjust sweetness by adding more powdered sugar if desired.
4. If the milkshake is too thick, you can add a little more brewed espresso or coffee, a tablespoon at a time, until you reach your desired consistency.
5. Once blended, pour the Tiramisu milkshake into chilled glasses.
6. If desired, top each milkshake with whipped cream and garnish with crushed ladyfingers, cocoa powder, or chocolate shavings.
7. Serve immediately with a straw and enjoy the decadent flavors of this Tiramisu Milkshake!

White Chocolate Raspberry Milkshake

Ingredients:

- 2 cups vanilla ice cream
- 1 cup frozen raspberries
- 1/2 cup white chocolate chips, melted and cooled
- 1 cup whole milk
- 2 tablespoons raspberry syrup or preserves
- Whipped cream (optional)
- Fresh raspberries for garnish (optional)
- White chocolate shavings for garnish (optional)

Instructions:

1. In a blender, combine the vanilla ice cream, frozen raspberries, melted white chocolate chips, whole milk, and raspberry syrup or preserves.
2. Blend on high speed until smooth and creamy, about 30-60 seconds.
3. If the milkshake is too thick, you can add a little more milk, a tablespoon at a time, until you reach your desired consistency.
4. Once blended, pour the White Chocolate Raspberry milkshake into chilled glasses.
5. If desired, top each milkshake with whipped cream and garnish with fresh raspberries and white chocolate shavings.
6. Serve immediately with a straw and enjoy the delicious combination of white chocolate and raspberry flavors in this White Chocolate Raspberry Milkshake!

Orange Creamsicle Milkshake

Ingredients:

- 2 cups vanilla ice cream
- 1 cup orange juice (freshly squeezed for best flavor)
- 1/4 cup milk (adjust for desired consistency)
- 1 tablespoon honey or sugar (adjust to taste)
- 1 teaspoon vanilla extract
- Zest of 1 orange (optional, for extra flavor)
- Whipped cream (optional)
- Orange slices for garnish (optional)

Instructions:

1. In a blender, combine the vanilla ice cream, orange juice, milk, honey or sugar, vanilla extract, and orange zest (if using).
2. Blend on high speed until smooth and creamy, about 30-60 seconds.
3. Taste and adjust sweetness by adding more honey or sugar if desired.
4. If the milkshake is too thick, you can add a little more milk, a tablespoon at a time, until you reach your desired consistency.
5. Once blended, pour the Orange Creamsicle milkshake into chilled glasses.
6. If desired, top each milkshake with whipped cream and garnish with orange slices.
7. Serve immediately with a straw and enjoy the refreshing and nostalgic flavors of this Orange Creamsicle Milkshake!

Eggnog Milkshake

Ingredients:

- 2 cups vanilla ice cream
- 1 cup eggnog
- 1/4 teaspoon ground cinnamon
- 1/8 teaspoon ground nutmeg
- 1/2 teaspoon vanilla extract
- Whipped cream (optional)
- Ground cinnamon or nutmeg for garnish (optional)

Instructions:

1. In a blender, combine the vanilla ice cream, eggnog, ground cinnamon, ground nutmeg, and vanilla extract.
2. Blend on high speed until smooth and creamy, about 30-60 seconds.
3. Taste and adjust the spice level by adding more ground cinnamon or nutmeg if desired.
4. If the milkshake is too thick, you can add a little more eggnog, a tablespoon at a time, until you reach your desired consistency.
5. Once blended, pour the Eggnog milkshake into chilled glasses.
6. If desired, top each milkshake with whipped cream and sprinkle with ground cinnamon or nutmeg for garnish.
7. Serve immediately with a straw and enjoy the festive and creamy flavors of this Eggnog Milkshake!

Honey Lavender Milkshake

Ingredients:

- 2 cups vanilla ice cream
- 1 cup whole milk
- 2 tablespoons honey
- 1 teaspoon culinary lavender buds
- 1/4 teaspoon vanilla extract
- Whipped cream (optional)
- Lavender flowers for garnish (optional)

Instructions:

1. In a small saucepan, heat the milk over medium heat until it just begins to simmer. Remove from heat.
2. Add the culinary lavender buds to the warm milk and let steep for about 5-10 minutes to infuse the flavor.
3. Strain the milk to remove the lavender buds and let it cool completely.
4. In a blender, combine the vanilla ice cream, cooled lavender-infused milk, honey, and vanilla extract.
5. Blend on high speed until smooth and creamy, about 30-60 seconds.
6. Taste and adjust sweetness by adding more honey if desired.
7. Once blended, pour the Honey Lavender milkshake into chilled glasses.
8. If desired, top each milkshake with whipped cream and garnish with lavender flowers.
9. Serve immediately with a straw and enjoy the delicate and floral flavors of this Honey Lavender Milkshake!

Caramel Macchiato Milkshake

Ingredients:

- 2 cups vanilla ice cream
- 1 cup brewed espresso or strong coffee, cooled
- 1/4 cup milk
- 2 tablespoons caramel sauce
- 1 tablespoon vanilla syrup
- Whipped cream (optional)
- Additional caramel sauce for drizzling (optional)

Instructions:

1. In a blender, combine the vanilla ice cream, brewed espresso or strong coffee, milk, caramel sauce, and vanilla syrup.
2. Blend on high speed until smooth and creamy, about 30-60 seconds.
3. Taste and adjust sweetness by adding more caramel sauce or vanilla syrup if desired.
4. If the milkshake is too thick, you can add a little more milk, a tablespoon at a time, until you reach your desired consistency.
5. Once blended, pour the Caramel Macchiato milkshake into chilled glasses.
6. If desired, top each milkshake with whipped cream and drizzle with additional caramel sauce.
7. Serve immediately with a straw and enjoy the rich and indulgent flavors of this Caramel Macchiato Milkshake!

Chocolate Covered Strawberry Milkshake

Ingredients:

- 2 cups vanilla ice cream
- 1 cup fresh strawberries, hulled and chopped
- 1/2 cup milk
- 2 tablespoons chocolate syrup
- 1 tablespoon cocoa powder
- Whipped cream (optional)
- Chocolate shavings or grated chocolate for garnish (optional)
- Fresh strawberries for garnish (optional)

Instructions:

1. In a blender, combine the vanilla ice cream, chopped strawberries, milk, chocolate syrup, and cocoa powder.
2. Blend on high speed until smooth and creamy, about 30-60 seconds.
3. If the milkshake is too thick, you can add a little more milk, a tablespoon at a time, until you reach your desired consistency.
4. Once blended, pour the Chocolate Covered Strawberry milkshake into chilled glasses.
5. If desired, top each milkshake with whipped cream and garnish with chocolate shavings or grated chocolate.
6. Add a fresh strawberry on the rim of each glass for an extra touch.
7. Serve immediately with a straw and enjoy the delightful combination of chocolate and strawberry flavors in this Chocolate Covered Strawberry Milkshake!

Maple Pecan Milkshake

Ingredients:

- 2 cups vanilla ice cream
- 1/2 cup milk
- 2 tablespoons maple syrup
- 1/4 cup chopped pecans, toasted
- 1/4 teaspoon vanilla extract
- Whipped cream (optional)
- Additional chopped pecans for garnish (optional)
- Maple syrup for drizzling (optional)

Instructions:

1. In a blender, combine the vanilla ice cream, milk, maple syrup, chopped pecans, and vanilla extract.
2. Blend on high speed until smooth and creamy, about 30-60 seconds.
3. If the milkshake is too thick, you can add a little more milk, a tablespoon at a time, until you reach your desired consistency.
4. Once blended, pour the Maple Pecan milkshake into chilled glasses.
5. If desired, top each milkshake with whipped cream and garnish with additional chopped pecans.
6. Drizzle with maple syrup for extra sweetness and flavor.
7. Serve immediately with a straw and enjoy the rich and nutty flavors of this Maple Pecan Milkshake!

Peppermint Patty Milkshake

Ingredients:

- 2 cups chocolate ice cream
- 1 cup milk
- 1/4 cup chocolate syrup
- 1/4 teaspoon peppermint extract
- 2 tablespoons crushed peppermint candies
- Whipped cream (optional)
- Additional crushed peppermint candies for garnish (optional)

Instructions:

1. In a blender, combine the chocolate ice cream, milk, chocolate syrup, peppermint extract, and crushed peppermint candies.
2. Blend on high speed until smooth and creamy, about 30-60 seconds.
3. If the milkshake is too thick, you can add a little more milk, a tablespoon at a time, until you reach your desired consistency.
4. Once blended, pour the Peppermint Patty milkshake into chilled glasses.
5. If desired, top each milkshake with whipped cream and garnish with additional crushed peppermint candies.
6. Serve immediately with a straw and enjoy the cool and refreshing flavors of this Peppermint Patty Milkshake!

Banana Split Milkshake

Ingredients:

- 2 ripe bananas, peeled and sliced
- 2 cups vanilla ice cream
- 1 cup whole milk
- 2 tablespoons chocolate syrup
- 2 tablespoons strawberry syrup
- 2 tablespoons pineapple syrup
- Whipped cream
- Maraschino cherries for garnish
- Chopped nuts (optional)

Instructions:

1. In a blender, combine the sliced bananas, vanilla ice cream, whole milk, and chocolate syrup.
2. Blend until smooth and creamy.
3. Pour the mixture evenly into three separate glasses.
4. Rinse the blender and then repeat the process, making one batch with the strawberry syrup and another with the pineapple syrup.
5. Layer each flavor on top of each other in the glasses.
6. Top each milkshake with whipped cream, a maraschino cherry, and chopped nuts if desired.
7. Serve immediately with a straw and enjoy the deliciousness of a classic banana split in milkshake form!

Blue Moon Milkshake

Ingredients:

- 2 cups vanilla ice cream
- 1/2 cup milk
- 1 tablespoon blue moon ice cream syrup (or blue curaçao syrup)
- 1/2 teaspoon vanilla extract
- Whipped cream (optional)
- Blue food coloring (optional)
- Sprinkles for garnish (optional)

Instructions:

1. In a blender, combine the vanilla ice cream, milk, blue moon ice cream syrup (or blue curaçao syrup), and vanilla extract.
2. If desired, add a drop or two of blue food coloring to enhance the blue color.
3. Blend until smooth and creamy.
4. Pour the milkshake into chilled glasses.
5. If desired, top each milkshake with whipped cream and sprinkle with colorful sprinkles.
6. Serve immediately with a straw and enjoy the whimsical and vibrant flavors of this Blue Moon Milkshake!

Lavender Honey Milkshake

Ingredients:

- 2 cups vanilla ice cream
- 1 cup milk
- 2 tablespoons honey
- 1 teaspoon culinary lavender buds
- 1/4 teaspoon vanilla extract
- Whipped cream (optional)
- Lavender sprigs for garnish (optional)

Instructions:

1. In a small saucepan, heat the milk over medium heat until it just begins to simmer. Remove from heat.
2. Add the culinary lavender buds to the warm milk and let steep for about 5-10 minutes to infuse the flavor.
3. Strain the milk to remove the lavender buds and let it cool completely.
4. In a blender, combine the vanilla ice cream, cooled lavender-infused milk, honey, and vanilla extract.
5. Blend on high speed until smooth and creamy, about 30-60 seconds.
6. Taste and adjust sweetness by adding more honey if desired.
7. Once blended, pour the Lavender Honey milkshake into chilled glasses.
8. If desired, top each milkshake with whipped cream and garnish with a lavender sprig.
9. Serve immediately with a straw and enjoy the delicate and aromatic flavors of this Lavender Honey Milkshake!

Irish Coffee Milkshake

Ingredients:

- 2 cups vanilla ice cream
- 1 cup cold brewed coffee
- 1/4 cup Irish cream liqueur (such as Baileys)
- 2 tablespoons chocolate syrup
- Whipped cream
- Cocoa powder or chocolate shavings for garnish (optional)

Instructions:

1. In a blender, combine the vanilla ice cream, cold brewed coffee, Irish cream liqueur, and chocolate syrup.
2. Blend until smooth and creamy.
3. Pour the milkshake into chilled glasses.
4. Top each milkshake with whipped cream.
5. Garnish with cocoa powder or chocolate shavings if desired.
6. Serve immediately with a straw and enjoy the rich and indulgent flavors of this Irish Coffee Milkshake!

www.ingramcontent.com/pod-product-compliance
Lightning Source LLC
LaVergne TN
LVHW081339060526
838201LV00055B/2741